THE STORY BEHIND

TOILETS

Elizabeth Raum

Heinemann Library
Chicago, Illinois

J
696.182
RAY

28

www.heinemannraintree.com
Visit our website to find out more information about Heinemann-Raintree books.

To order:
☎ Phone 888-454-2279
💻 Visit www.heinemannraintree.com to browse our catalog and order online.

Edited by Louise Galpine, Megan Cotugno, and Laura Knowles
Designed by Philippa Jenkins and Artistix
Original illustrations © Capstone Global Library, LLC 2009
Illustrated by Tony Wilson, p. 5; Phil Gleaves/Specs Art pp. 6, 14, 18; Darren Lingard, p. 10
Picture research by Mica Brancic and Elaine Willis
Originated by Modern Age Repro House Ltd.
Printed in China by CTPS

13 12 11 10 09
10 9 8 7 6 5 4 3 2

Library of Congress Cataloging-in-Publication Data
Raum, Elizabeth.
  The story behind toilets / Elizabeth Raum.
    p. cm. -- (True stories)
  Includes bibliographical references and index.
  ISBN 978-1-4329-2350-1 (hc)
  1. Toilets--History--Juvenile literature. I. Title.
  GT476.R38 2008
  696'.182--dc22

                          2008037392

Acknowledgments
The author and publishers are grateful to the following for permission to reproduce copyright material: Alamy p. **4** (© Richard Heyes); © Bridgeman Art Library p. **12** (Guildhall Library, City of London); Corbis pp. **7** (© Roger Wood), **8** (© Bob Krist), **11** (© Bettmann), **13** (© Leonard de Selva), **19** (© epa), **20** (zefa/© Mika), **27** (© Reuters/David Gray); Getty Images pp. **15** (Look/© Franz Marc Frei), **16** (Stringer/© Jeff T. Green), **21** (Stone/© Robert Holmgren), **22** (© Scott Olson); © Incinolet p. **24**; © Mary Evans Picture Library 2008 p. **17**; Science Photo Library pp. **23** (© MARK SYKES), **25** (© ALAN SIRULNIKOFF), **26** (© NASA); Shutterstock p. **iii** (© Morgan Lane Photography); Topfoto p. **9** (© Fotomas).

Cover photograph reproduced with permission of Photolibrary Group (Blend Images).

Every effort has been made to contact copyright holders of any material reproduced in this book. Any omissions will be rectified in subsequent printings if notice is given to the publisher.

All the Internet addresses (URLs) given in this book were valid at the time of going to press. However, due to the dynamic nature of the Internet, some addresses may have changed, or sites may have changed or ceased to exist since publication. While the author and Publishers regret any inconvenience this may cause readers, no responsibility for any such changes can be accepted by either the author or the Publishers.

Contents

■ **Potty Talk**. 4

■ **A Short History of Toilets**. 6

■ **Sewers** 12

■ **Cleaning Up** 16

■ **No Place to Go**. 18

■ **Saving Water** 22

■ **Toilets for Tomorrow** 26

■ *Timeline* 28

■ *Glossary* 30

■ *Find Out More* 31

■ *Index*. 32

Some words are shown in bold, **like this**.
You can find out what they mean by
looking in the glossary.

Potty Talk

▲ People usually sit down when they use American- and European-style toilets like this one.

Whether they stand up, squat, or sit down, all people need toilets. When people eat and drink, their bodies use what they need and then get rid of the rest as waste. Liquid waste is called **urine**. Solid waste is called **excrement**.

In the United States, people say they go to the restroom or bathroom to get rid of bodily waste. In England, people say they go to the toilet, lavatory, WC (meaning "water closet"), or loo. In past times, toilets were called privies. Toilets outside the house are called outhouses, necessary houses, or **latrines**. Toilets, no matter what they are called, are an important part of daily life.

▶ **This diagram shows the major parts of the body used in digestion.**

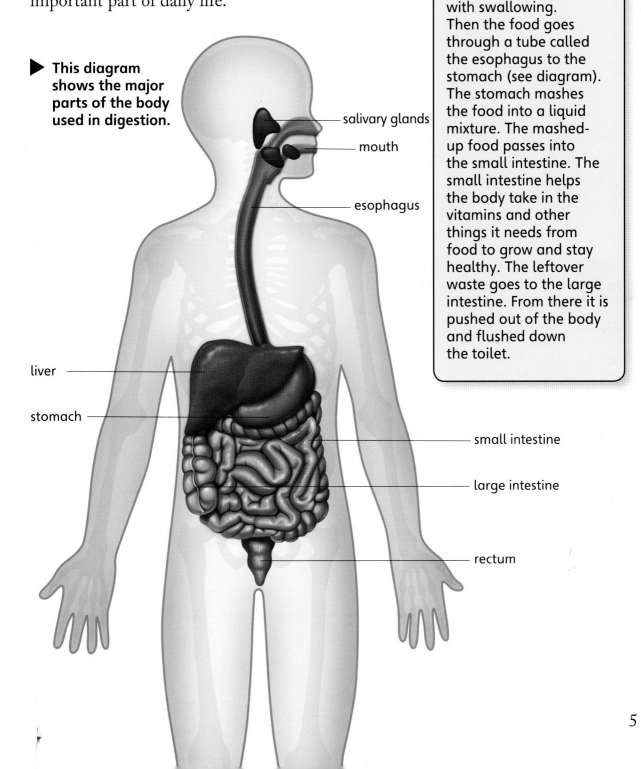

salivary glands

mouth

esophagus

liver

stomach

small intestine

large intestine

rectum

Digestion

Digestion is the process that lets the body get vitamins and energy from food. When people eat, the saliva in the mouth softens the food. This helps with swallowing. Then the food goes through a tube called the esophagus to the stomach (see diagram). The stomach mashes the food into a liquid mixture. The mashed-up food passes into the small intestine. The small intestine helps the body take in the vitamins and other things it needs from food to grow and stay healthy. The leftover waste goes to the large intestine. From there it is pushed out of the body and flushed down the toilet.

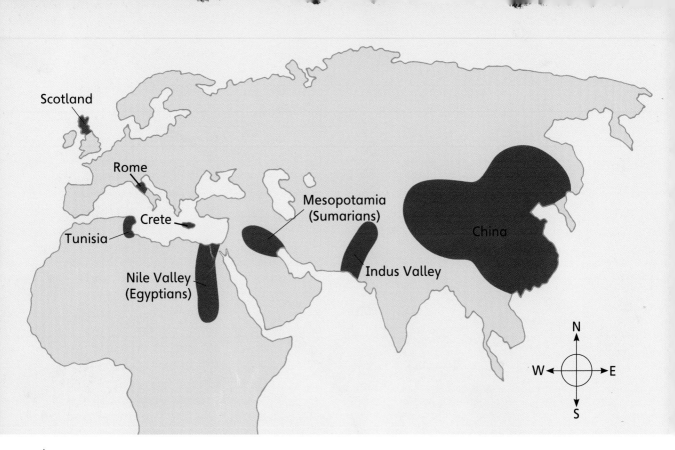

Scotland

Rome

Crete

Tunisia

Nile Valley
(Egyptians)

Mesopotamia
(Sumarians)

China

Indus Valley

N
W ← → E
S

▲ **This map shows
the places in the
ancient world that
developed toilets.**

Early people did not live in towns or villages. Instead, they camped in one place for a while. Then they moved on. They left their waste behind. But as people began to live in communities, they had to find another way to deal with human waste.

At first ancient people dug holes for waste or used pots that had to be emptied. In about 2500 BCE (4,500 years ago) ancient communities in Scotland and in the Indus Valley (present-day Pakistan) used a system of pipes to carry waste outside from indoor toilets. At about the same time, the king of Sumer in Mesopotamia built six toilets in his palace.

2500 BCE
Toilets exist in Mesopotamia, the Indus Valley, and Scotland.

2000 BCE
Flush toilets are used in Crete.

3000 BCE

2000 BCE

Other ancient toilets

Toilets in ancient Egypt had a keyhole shape to make them comfortable. A pot beneath the seat was filled with sand. Human waste fell into the sand and was emptied by a servant. Later, the Romans (who lived in present-day Italy) built **sewer** systems. The sewers carried waste from toilets into nearby streams and rivers.

Flush toilets

The palace of Knossos, built about 2000 BCE (4,000 years ago) on the island of Crete, had the first toilets that flushed. Pans on the roof of the palace collected rainwater. Pipes slowly carried the rainwater to the toilets, washing away waste. A wooden seat covered the drain system. The seat also kept the person using it dry.

▼ There are places for twelve men to use this toilet at one time. It was built between 100 and 200 CE in Tunisia in Africa.

▶ This U.S. chamber pot from the 1700s is decorated with the face of Great Britain's King George III.

Chamber pots

Rich Egyptians, Greeks, and Romans chose to use jars or pots as toilets. These were called **chamber pots**. Poor people simply went outside. If they were too sick to go outside, they used clay pots.

Middle Ages

During the Middle Ages (500 CE to 1450 CE), almost all flush toilets and sewer systems disappeared. People either went outside or used chamber pots.

Castles often had **garderobes**. These were small seats built into a tiny closet hanging over the castle's **moat**. Waste ran down the castle wall into the moat. Moats full of **sewage** smelled terrible.

In the 1500s, rich people used fancy chamber pots called **close stools**. Many were made to look like a box. The lid opened to show a seat decorated in velvet and lace. Beneath the seat was a pot to catch waste.

500–1450
Chamber pots and garderobes are in use. Flush toilets disappear.

1500s
Close stools are used.

City problems

Before the 1600s, most people lived on farms or in small villages. Waste was not a problem. But as people moved to crowded cities, the problem of human waste grew. People urinated in the streets. They also emptied chamber pots onto the streets. Farmers collected some of the waste to spread on their fields as a **fertilizer**. The rest of the waste ran into rivers and **wells**. This made the water unsafe to drink.

◄ Chamber pots used to be dumped onto the street.

1600   1700   1800

► This diagram shows how a toilet works. When the toilet handle is pushed, water rushes from the tank into the bowl. This forces the water and waste in the bowl to empty into the sewer drain. When the water level in the tank drains, a stopper opens. The tank refills with water.

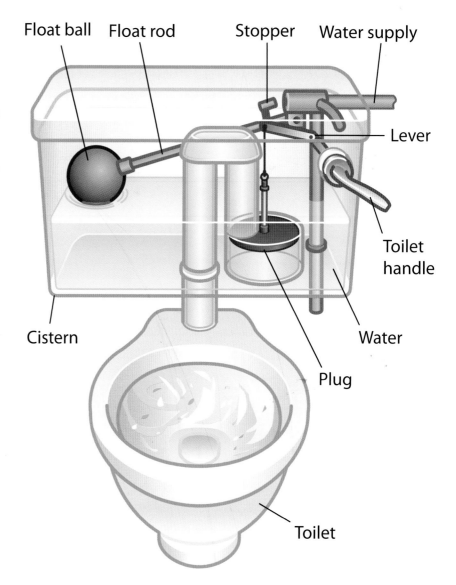

Float ball   Float rod   Stopper   Water supply

Lever

Toilet handle

Cistern

Water

Plug

Toilet

Modern flush toilets

In 1590 English inventor Sir John Harington designed a flush toilet. He put it in his own home. A tank near the ceiling released water when the toilet's handle was pulled. England's Queen Elizabeth I put one in her palace. Few others were willing to try it. In fact, they made fun of Harington's flush toilet.

1590
English inventor
Sir John Harington
invents the flush toilet.

1738
French architect
J. F. Blondel
improves the toilet.

People continued to use outhouses or chamber pots until French architect J. F. Blondel made a better flush toilet in 1738. This toilet included a flap, or valve, to keep odors out of the house. By the 1770s, people in Great Britain and France began putting flush toilets inside their homes. In 1870 Englishman S. S. Hellyer invented a flush toilet similar to the one people use today.

Until this time in the United States, many people did not have running water in their homes. Without running water, they could not use flush toilets. It was not until about 1870 that most U.S. homes had indoor plumbing and flush toilets.

CRAPPER'S

Improved

Registered Ornamental

Flush-down W.C.

With New Design Cast-iron Syphon Water Waste Preventer.

No 518.

Improved Ornamental Flush-down W.C. Basin (Registered No. 145,823), Polished Mahogany Seat with flap, New Pattern 3-gallon Cast-iron Syphon Cistern (Rd. No. 149,284), Brass Flushing Pipe and Clips, and Pendant Pull, complete as shown £6 15 0

◄ Crapper's toilets had better flush systems than earlier toilets. This advertisement shows that they were also very decorative.

Thomas Crapper's toilet ✔

In 1884 English plumber Thomas Crapper designed a toilet that flushed more easily. Thomas Crapper & Company made many of the toilets used in Europe. Great Britain's Queen Victoria honored him, but U.S. soldiers made him famous. U.S. soldiers working in England during World War I (1914–18) began to call toilets 'crappers.'

1770s
The British and French add indoor toilets to buildings.

1870
Englishman S. S. Hellyer invents the modern flush toilet. Americans add indoor toilets to buildings.

1884
English plumber Thomas Crapper improves the toilet.

1800

1900

Sewers

▲ This 1854 drawing shows workmen repairing London's Fleet Street sewer.

By the 1840s most cities had **sewer** problems. As more people used flush toilets, sewers could not handle the waste. Sewers overflowed. People became sick when **sewage** leaked into drinking water.

In London, England, human waste drained into the Fleet River and the Thames River. The rivers were clogged by waste, dead dogs, dead cats, and rats. Vegetables, kettles, broken pots, and all kinds of trash filled the sewers.

1858
London, England, experiences "the Great Stink."

1859
London repairs its sewers.

1800   1850

The summer of 1858 was called "the Great Stink." Even members of the government left town to avoid the smell. It took years to fix the sewers. When the sewer system was finished, the stink went away. City dwellers then lived longer and had fewer diseases.

Sewage treatment

Even after the London sewers were repaired, waste still emptied into the Thames River. Most cities drained sewage into rivers. But human waste kills fish and clogs rivers. In 1890 some cities began to use filters and **chemicals** to treat the waste before putting it back into rivers and lakes.

In 1916 two U.S. scientists first treated waste with **bacteria** before returning it to rivers or lakes. Many cities continue to use this system today.

Sewers of Paris

By 1878 the sewers of Paris, France, were 580 kilometers (360 miles) long. People enjoyed touring the sewers in carts pushed by workers. Later they used small trains and boats. Today, Paris's sewers cover 2,100 kilometers (1,300 miles). They remain open for tours.

▼ **Tours of Paris sewers were popular in 1870, when this drawing was made.**

1890
Chemicals are used to treat waste.

1916
Bacteria are used to treat waste.

1900

1950

Sewage today

People who live in the country use big tanks buried in the yard for sewage treatment. Waste drains from the house into these **septic tanks.** Over time, the waste breaks down. The **wastewater** flows into the ground through a **drain field**.

▶ **This diagram shows how a septic system works. The scum layer breaks down into water and sludge. The system must be cleaned from time to time.**

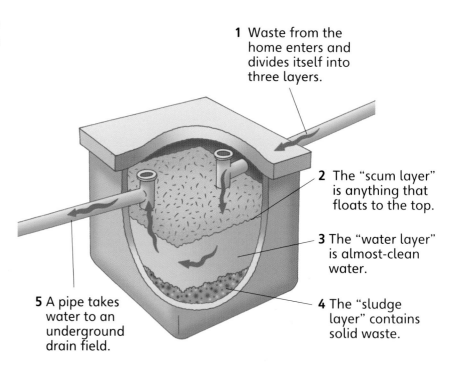

1 Waste from the home enters and divides itself into three layers.

2 The "scum layer" is anything that floats to the top.

3 The "water layer" is almost-clean water.

4 The "sludge layer" contains solid waste.

5 A pipe takes water to an underground drain field.

City and town systems

Cities and towns need larger sewer systems than septic tanks. Pipes carry waste from homes and businesses to a large pipe called a sewer main. The sewer main runs beneath the streets. Workers check the sewer mains by going down a **manhole**.

Large tanks collect waste from the sewer main. Liquid waste is separated from solid waste. Solid waste is burned or spread on farm fields as a **fertilizer**. The liquid waste is treated with a gas called chlorine and with bacteria. Then the treated waste is returned to nearby lakes and rivers.

Reed beds

Another system for treating wastewater is called reed-bed technology. This system uses tall grasses (called reeds) that grow in wet areas. Pipes carry sewage to the reed beds. In time the wastewater evaporates (turns into a gas). Then bacteria at the roots of the reeds break down the solid waste.

▲ This large sewage treatment plant in Munich, Germany, has many tanks for treating sewage.

Flower helpers

In 1989 National Aeronautics and Space Administration (NASA) scientists began using flowering water plants to clean wastewater. They used hyacinths, lilies, and others. Flowering plants take in waste gases and give off clean air. Later, the scientists crushed the plants and used them as fertilizer to grow corn, tomatoes, potatoes, cucumbers, and squash.

15

Cleaning Up

▲ This giant roll of paper will be made into a special kind of toilet paper for **septic tanks**. It breaks down about 30 seconds after flushing.

Toilet paper was first sold in the United States in 1857. It was sold in Great Britain from about 1863. At first, people felt embarrassed about buying toilet paper. Companies sold it in plain wrappers. As time went on, toilet paper became an everyday item. Today, people would not want to live without it.

1400s
The Chinese make the first toilet paper.

1500s
Rich Europeans use paper from books for toilet paper.

1400   1500   1600

Before toilet paper

Ancient Romans used a sponge on the end of a stick to clean up after using the toilet. When finished, they put the sponge in a pail full of water so that the next person could use it. Other early people used water to clean up. Some used stones, sand, or seashells to scrape themselves clean.

In the United States, people used corncobs dipped in water as toilet paper. They kept a basket of corncobs in the outhouse. After use, they tossed the corncobs into the pit of the outhouse.

Big business

In 2005, $5.7 billion worth of toilet paper was sold in the United States alone.

The first toilet papers

The Chinese were the first to use soft toilet paper. In about 1400 CE they were making 720,000 sheets of toilet paper a year to be used by royalty. In Europe in the late 1500s, rich people took a book to the toilet. They ripped out pages to use for cleaning themselves. Poorer people used bits of paper bags, ads, and newspapers.

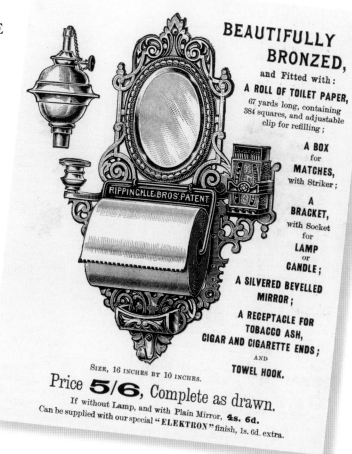

BEAUTIFULLY BRONZED,
and Fitted with:
A ROLL OF TOILET PAPER,
67 yards long, containing
384 squares, and adjustable
clip for refilling;

A BOX
for
MATCHES,
with Striker;

A
BRACKET,
with Socket
for
LAMP
or
CANDLE;

A SILVERED BEVELLED
MIRROR;

A RECEPTACLE FOR
TOBACCO ASH,
CIGAR AND CIGARETTE ENDS;
AND
TOWEL HOOK.

SIZE, 16 INCHES BY 10 INCHES.

Price **5/6**, Complete as drawn.
If without Lamp, and with Plain Mirror, **4s. 6d.**
Can be supplied with our special "ELEKTRON" finish, 1s. 6d. extra.

RIPPINGILLE BROS' PATENT

▶ This early toilet paper holder also included a candle holder, towel hook, and mirror.

1857	1863
Toilet paper is sold in the United States.	Toilet paper is sold in Great Britain.

1700　　　1800　　　1900

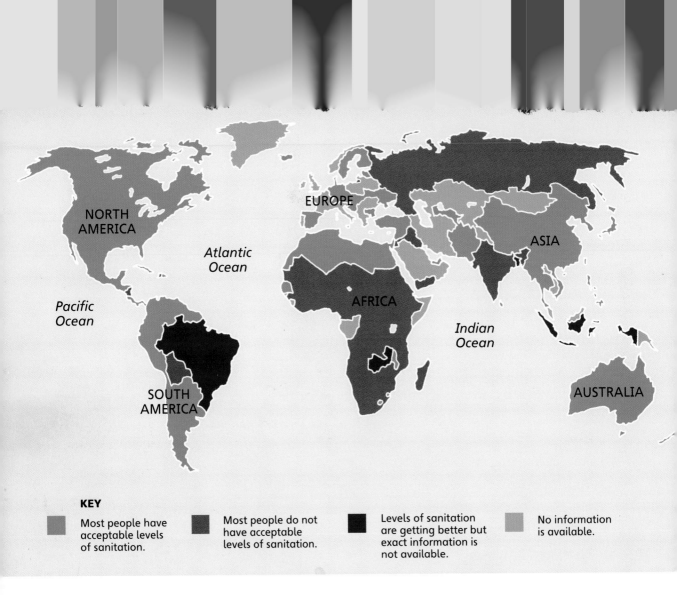

NORTH
AMERICA

Atlantic
Ocean

EUROPE

ASIA

Pacific
Ocean

AFRICA

Indian
Ocean

SOUTH
AMERICA

AUSTRALIA

KEY

Most people have acceptable levels of sanitation.

Most people do not have acceptable levels of sanitation.

Levels of sanitation are getting better but exact information is not available.

No information is available.

▲ **This world map shows the progress of different regions toward acceptable levels of sanitation.**

People in North America and Europe usually take toilets and toilet paper for granted. But in many parts of the world, there are not enough toilets. Today, 2.6 billion people do not have proper toilets and **sewer** systems.

Health dangers

Without toilets and sewer systems, human waste may wash into nearby **wells** or streams used as drinking water. Drinking untreated **wastewater** is very dangerous for babies and young children. Nearly 1.6 million children under the age of five die every year because of poor **sanitation**.

International Year of Sanitation

The United Nations (UN) named 2008 the International Year of Sanitation. One of the UN's goals is to provide safe toilets for everyone in the world by 2025. UN experts say that it will take $10 billion a year to reach their goal. Americans spend four times that much each year on their pets. People in Europe spend that much on ice cream each year. Money for toilets will save lives.

Toilet house

In 2007 a Korean lawmaker named Sim Jae-duck built a house shaped like a toilet. He called his house *Haewoojae*, which means "a place where one can solve one's worries." The house has four toilets. The one in the center of the house is see-through. A special system fogs the glass whenever someone uses the toilet. Jae-duck built the house because he worried about the worldwide lack of proper toilets. He wants people to work on the problem.

▼ This Korean house looks like a giant toilet.

Pay toilets

Where do people "go" when they are away from home? Restaurants and stores provide free restrooms. But what if people do not want to eat or shop? Many people believe that every city and town should provide public restrooms that are free, clean, and safe.

Others say that it costs too much to provide free restrooms. Until the 1970s, pay toilets were common in the United States. Recently, New York City and Pittsburgh, Pennsylvania, installed public toilets. They cost 25 cents per use. The money is used to keep toilets clean and safe.

▶ It is expensive to keep public toilets clean and in good working order.

Portable toilets

Portable toilets can be delivered to where they are needed. They can be used at fairs, music festivals, and building sites. Waste collects in a tank beneath the seat. A **sewage** truck collects the waste. The truck takes it to a sewage treatment plant. After the toilets are cleaned, they can be used again or moved to a new location.

▼ National parks and tourist attractions may provide portable toilets like these, which are used in Colorado.

Saving Water

▶ Waterless urinals like this have been in use throughout the world for a number of years.

People flush a lot of water down the toilet. In Europe and North America, most of the water used in houses is used in bathrooms. Much of the water is used for flushing. Toilets made before 1982 use between 19 and 27 liters (5 and 7 gallons) of water per flush. New low-flow toilets use between 4.8 and 6 liters (1.3 and 1.6 gallons) per flush.

Waterless urinals

Some **urinals** need no water. A waterless urinal has an odor trap made of natural vegetable oil. Since the **urine** is heavier than the oil, it passes through directly into the **sewer** system. The urinal is sprayed with a cleaner once a month. Replacing older toilets at home with these will help reduce water use.

Dual-flush toilets

Dual-flush toilets also help reduce water use. One button uses less water to flush urine. The other uses more to flush **excrement**. All new buildings in Ireland must use dual-flush toilets to save water. Australia also wants people to use dual-flush models.

◀ A dual-flush toilet has two buttons. One uses less water to flush urine. The other uses more water to flush solid waste.

▶ This toilet uses gas or electricity to burn waste. It does not require any water to work.

Environmentally friendly latrines ✓

The government of Malawi, Africa, is building special latrines for toddlers and young children. Workers dig small pits behind bushes for children. When the pit is full, workers plant a tree in the full latrine and dig a new pit for children to use.

Latrines

Lack of water is a problem throughout the world. **Latrines** work well in areas without water systems. Latrines are the most common **sanitation** system in the world. People build latrines outside by digging a deep hole and placing a support over the hole. Latrines should be far from **wells** and streams used as drinking water. Waste collects in the pit. When it is full, the pit is filled with dirt. A new latrine is dug nearby. Most outhouses are latrines with covers.

Compost toilets

Compost toilets also work well in areas without a lot of water. They are sometimes used for camping, on boats, or in homes without running water. A compost toilet breaks waste down into something called humus. Humus can be spread on soil to make the soil richer for growing crops. It is safe and will not cause disease. Compost toilets cost less than flush toilets. They save water.

▼ A compost toilet works without water or a sewer system.

Toilets for Tomorrow

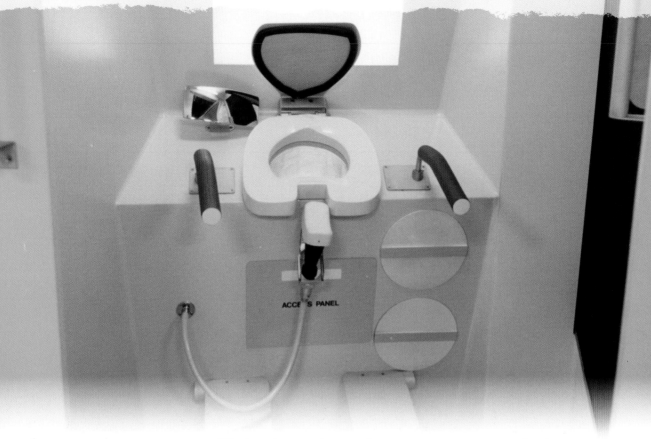

▲ The International Space Station will soon use a toilet-to-tap system.

Toilets have changed in many ways over the last 4,000 years. So has the way people use water and treat human waste.

Recycling wastewater

About 15 cities and towns in the United States now use a "toilet-to-tap" system. It turns **wastewater** into drinking water. After the waste is treated, the water is safe to drink.

El Paso, Texas and Orange County, California are currently using toilet-to-tap systems. The Orange County program treats wastewater for up to two years. Then it is returned as drinking water. This same system will soon be used on the International Space Station.

Urine

Urine is 95 percent pure water. The other 5 percent is made up of salt, ammonia, and other natural **chemicals**. These chemicals must be removed before urine is safe to drink. Drinking untreated urine is not safe!

Some people say "yuck!" to the idea of toilet-to-tap systems. People in San Diego and Los Angeles, California, rejected the new system. But experts say that in time people everywhere will accept the idea of using cleaned wastewater for cooking and drinking.

▼ In November 2000, workers in Sydney, Australia, found this American alligator snapping turtle in the sewer. Animal experts think it was stolen from a reptile park 21 years earlier and then wandered into the sewer.

Alligators? ✔

In 1935 an alligator fell off a boat into New York's East River and swam into the **sewer** system. It was captured. People began to make up frightening stories about other alligators living in the sewers.

Timeline

(These dates are often approximations.)

2500 BCE
Toilets exist in Mesopotamia, the Indus Valley, and Scotland.

3000 BCE

1400s
The Chinese make the first toilet paper.

1400

1600s–1800s
Cities grow; so do waste problems.

1738
French architect J. F. Blondel improves the toilet.

1700

1884
English plumber Thomas Crapper improves and sells toilets.

1870
Englishman S. S. Hellyer invents the modern flush toilet. Americans add indoor toilets to buildings.

1863
Toilet paper is sold in Great Britain.

1890
Chemicals are used to treat waste.

1916
Bacteria are used to treat waste.

1900

This symbol shows where there is a change of scale in the timeline, or where a long period of time with no noted events has been left out.

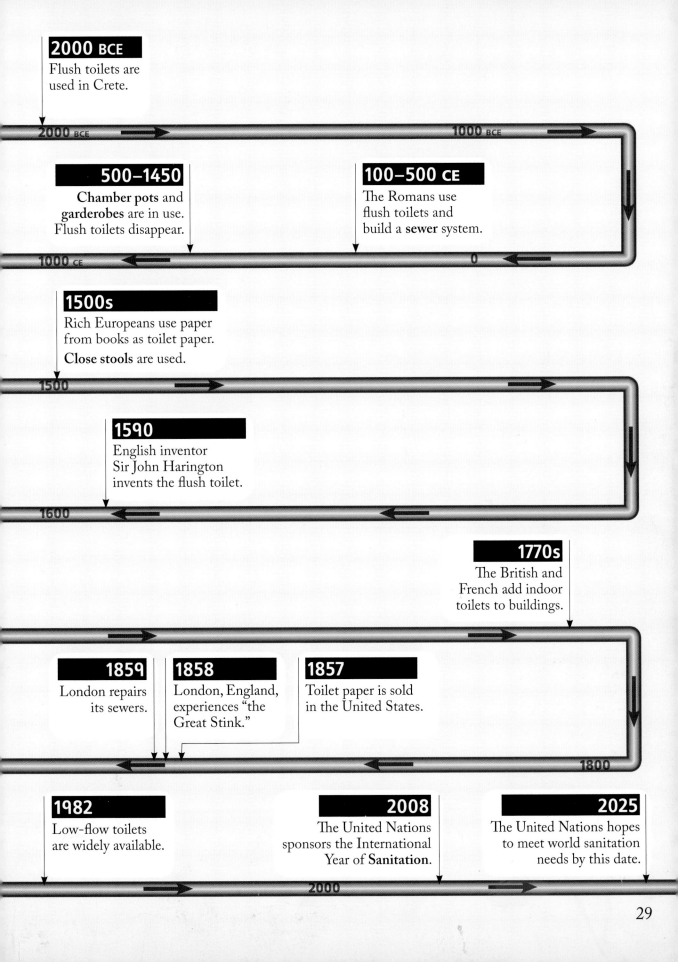

2000 BCE
Flush toilets are used in Crete.

2000 BCE   1000 BCE

500–1450
Chamber pots and **garderobes** are in use. Flush toilets disappear.

100–500 CE
The Romans use flush toilets and build a **sewer** system.

1000 CE   0

1500s
Rich Europeans use paper from books as toilet paper.
Close stools are used.

1500

1590
English inventor Sir John Harington invents the flush toilet.

1600

1770s
The British and French add indoor toilets to buildings.

1859
London repairs its sewers.

1858
London, England, experiences "the Great Stink."

1857
Toilet paper is sold in the United States.

1800

1982
Low-flow toilets are widely available.

2008
The United Nations sponsors the International Year of **Sanitation**.

2025
The United Nations hopes to meet world sanitation needs by this date.

2000

Glossary

bacterium (more than one: **bacteria**) tiny living thing that can be used to treat sewage. Some bacteria cause disease, but others are used to treat sewage.

BCE meaning "before the common era." When this appears after a date, it refers to the time before the Christian religion began. BCE dates are always counted backwards.

CE meaning "common era." When this appears after a date, it refers to the time after the Christian religion began.

chamber pot jug or pot used as a toilet. Some chamber pots were simple, but others had fancy decorations.

chemical something used to remove dangerous germs from wastewater. Chemicals help treat sewage.

close stool fancy kind of chamber pot used by the wealthy in the 1500s. The seats of close stools featured decorations in fine materials such as velvet and lace.

drain field area of soil surrounding a septic tank. The drain field soaks up liquid waste from the septic tank.

excrement waste matter discharged from the body. Sewage treatment plants separate excrement from liquid waste.

fertilizer something that makes soil produce better crops. It is safe to use human waste as fertilizer.

garderobe toilet built into the wall of a castle that drained into the moat. Garderobes were cold and drafty in winter.

latrine trench dug into the ground and used as a toilet. During wars, soldiers build latrines near their camps.

manhole covered opening in the street that leads to sewer pipes. Workers climb down manholes to check the sewers.

moat water surrounding a castle. In past times, people in castles drained sewage into the moat.

sanitation method of dealing with human waste or sewage. Everyone in the world needs good sanitation.

septic tank system for treating waste in areas without sewer lines. Some people who live in the country use septic tanks.

sewage human waste. Sewage goes through pipes into the sewer system.

sewer pipe used for carrying away sewage. Most cities and towns have a sewer system.

urinal toilet used for liquid waste that is attached to a wall. Urinals are found in men's restrooms.

urine liquid human waste.

wastewater water that has been used for washing, flushing, or in manufacturing; also called sewage. Wastewater must be treated at a sewage treatment plant before it is returned to rivers or lakes.

well hole dug in the earth in order to get water. Sewage should be kept away from wells.

Find Out More

Books

Barnhill, Kelly Regan. *Sewers and the Rats That Love Them: The Disgusting Story Behind Where It All Goes*. Mankato, Minn.: Capstone, 2009.

Harper, Charise Mericle. *Flush!: The Scoop on Poop Throughout the Ages*. New York: Little Brown, 2007.

Miller, Connie C. *Getting to Know Your Toilet: The Disgusting Story Behind Your Home's Strangest Feature*. Mankato, Minn.: Capstone, 2009.

Websites

Visit the website of the International Year of Sanitation.
http://esa.un.org/iys/

Visit the website of the Museum of Toilets.
www.sulabhtoiletmuseum.org/pg01.htm

Play Ain't So Stinky sewer games.
www.sandiego.gov/mwwd/kids/learnit/games.shtml

Learn more about decorated toilets.
www.victoriancrapper.com

Places to visit

Visit your city's or town's water department. Perhaps you can tour the sewer system.

Index

American Revolution 8
ammonia 27
ancient world 6–7
Australia 23, 27

bacteria 13, 14
Blondel, J.F. 11

chamber pots 8, 9, 11
chemicals 13, 27
chlorine 14
close stools 8
compost toilets 25
corncobs 17
Crapper, Thomas 11
Crete 7

digestion 5
diseases 12, 13, 18, 25
drain fields 14
drinking water 12, 18, 24, 26
dual-flush toilets 23

Egypt 7
Elizabeth I, Queen of England 10
England 5, 10, 11, 12–13, 20
excrement 4, 8, 23

fertilizer 9, 14, 15
filters 13
flush toilets 7, 8, 11
    dual-flush toilets 23
    earliest 7
    how a toilet works 10
    low-flow toilets 23
    water usage 23
France 11, 13

garderobes 8
George III, King of England 8
Great Stink (1858) 13

Harington, Sir John 10
Hellyer, S.S. 11
humus 25

incinerating toilets 24
Indus valley 6
International Space Station 26
International Year of Sanitation 19
Ireland 23

Knossos 7

latrines 5, 24
    environmentally friendly 24
lavatories 5
loos 5

Malawi 24
manholes 14
Mesopotamia 6
Middle Ages 8
moats 8

National Aeronautics and Space Administration (NASA) 15
necessary houses 5

odors 8, 11, 13
odor trap 11, 23
outhouses 5, 11, 17, 24

Paris 13
pay toilets 20
pop-up toilets 20
portable toilets 21
privies 5
public toilets 20

recycled toilet bowls 23
reed-bed technology 15

restrooms 5, 20
rivers 9, 12, 13, 14
Romans 7, 8, 17

sanitation
    global levels of 18
    most common system 24
    poor 18
Scotland 6
septic tanks 14, 16
sewage 8, 12, 13, 14
sewage systems 8, 12–15, 18
    animals in 27
    flowering plants, use of 15
    pipes 6, 7, 14, 15
    reed-bed technology 15
    Roman 7
    septic tanks 14
    tours of 13
    treatment plants 15, 21
sewage trucks 21
sewer mains 14
Sim Jae-duck 19
sponges 17

toilet house 19
toilet paper 16, 17
toilet paper holders 17
toilet-to-tap system 26–27
toilets 5
    compost toilets 25
    flush toilets 7, 8, 10, 11, 23
    history of toilets 6–11
    incinerating toilets 24
    pay toilets 20
    portable toilets 21

Tunisia 7

United Nations (UN) 19
United States 5, 8, 11, 16, 20, 26, 27
urinals
    odor trap 23
    pop-up 20
    waterless 22, 23
urine 4, 23, 27
    drinking 27

Victoria, Queen of England 11

waste 4, 5, 6, 7, 8, 9, 12, 13, 21
    liquid 4, 14
    solid 4, 14
wastewater 14, 15, 19
    recycled 26–27
water saving 22–23, 25
WC 5
wells 9, 18, 24